Strike
a Giant Bell

Gifts of
Pope John Paul II

Strike a Giant Bell

Gifts of Pope John Paul II

By
Rev. Msgr. John F. Davis

ST. PAUL EDITIONS

NIHIL OBSTAT:
    Rev. Richard V. Lawlor, S.J.

IMPRIMATUR:
    + Humberto Cardinal Medeiros
    Archbishop of Boston

PHOTO CREDITS:

Fabian Bachrach — 10
Felici — 6, 1,14, 133
Arturo Mari — 29, 59, 63, 71, 80, 82, 108, 117, 128
Chris Sheridan — 33, 92
UPI — 110

ISBN 0-8198-6815-9 (cloth)
    0-8198-6816-7 (paper)

Printed in the U.S.A. by the Daughters of St. Paul
50 St. Paul's Ave., Boston, MA 02130

The Daughters of St. Paul are an international congregation
of religious women serving the Church with the communi-
cations media.

"In the middle of all their quarrels
God will strike a giant bell
for a Slavonic Pope."

Julius Slowacki, 1848

TO HIS HOLINESS
POPE JOHN PAUL II
265TH VICAR OF CHRIST ON EARTH

*"Blessed are you who come to us
in the name of the Lord."*

+ Humberto Cardinal Medeiros
Archbishop of Boston

IN MEMORY OF
MY BELOVED PARENTS
FRANK AND AMELIA

CONTENTS

Section Three
THE HEART OF THE POPE

Section Four
THE MIND OF THE POPE

Section Five
THE JOURNEY OF THE POPE

Preface

This is my second book. The first, having the title *This Priest Is Thankful,* recounted various influences in my life. The epilogue of that book was a chapter devoted to Pope John Paul II. I knew then that my second book would treat in greater scope the tremendous influence of Pope John Paul II on my life and on my priesthood.

This book begins where that first one concluded. I would not attempt an actual detailed biography of the Holy Father; there are many excellent ones from well-informed sources. Here I mean to discuss how much the Pope has meant to me, to the strengthening of the priesthood, and to those who were beginning to feel like strangers in their own Church.

All persons may identify with the constant surprises that God's goodness sends. God is a God of surprises and as the economy of salvation unfolds, when hope is running out, He gives "a surprise Pope."

SECTION ONE

The Pope as Priest

1 The Surprise on the Balcony

It is no secret that I am a fervent Wojtylan. Ever since that October 16th evening when Karol Wojtyla stood on the middle balcony of St. Peter's Basilica in Rome as Pope John Paul II, I have been a different priest.

That night was a surprise to the world. For 450 years the Popes had been Italian. There had never been a Polish Pope. Nor did anyone think it was likely to be other than an Italian. Even some of the Cardinals had mentioned that fact shortly before their Conclave. Not many of us had heard of Cardinal Wojtyla although perhaps we should have, as his career and travels had brought him to our country. He merited our attention as a scholar. Evidently, the Cardinals had been impressed by his person perhaps much more than we knew.

Only a month before, Pope John Paul I, previously Archbishop of Venice, had been the choice of the Cardinals. After his sudden death, many names were prominently featured in the media. When I first heard the announcement of the new Pope, I couldn't believe it. Within minutes it was fact. When John Paul II came out on the balcony, awe, serenity, and peace commingled as he, the first Polish Pope, spoke in fluent Italian to those standing below in the Square, in the embrace of the Bernini columns. And there were millions who were also "there" via television.

What a marvelous approach to the city of Rome and to the world by the new Pope, one called from a distant country! After a period of some confusion, unrest and uncertainty, God had worked an unfathomable miracle. For me, it was the return of faith and hope. Charity is the last always to leave. Why had we doubted when God had promised His assistance forever and when He had saved the Church in far worse crises of faith?

The surprise Pope broke tradition by giving a talk at his first appearance. They say he did this on his own, disregarding protocol. Then to speak in "our" Italian language, to assert that he had come from a far country yet near to Rome in faith and loyalty to the See of Peter, to mention the

Madonna three times in the first few words, to speak of starting anew on the road of history—in a forceful language and strong voice—we had a Pope!

At the first announcement, the throng in the Square was surprised as we all were. Some registered disappointment evidenced by the weakness of their reaction to the "foreign" name of "Wojtyla." After the Pope had spoken, within those few minutes, the inevitable happened. If ever God was in a man, here was that man! There was applause, then smiles, then tears. I, too, had each of these emotions. We immediately loved him and, we knelt and received his first blessing as Pope. We prayed for him as a symbol of unity, faith, and strength for our Church.

John XXIII and Paul VI now had their spiritual son in the Chair of Peter. John XXIII had known him as a bishop. Paul VI, who had known him well from his student priest days, had conferred upon him the Cardinalate, knowing thereby that he could some day become Pope. So John Paul II took his Predecessors' names, as had John Paul I. John is the name of the apostle whom Jesus loved. Paul is the name of the first protagonist for the Faith. The new Pope would embody the apostle John's love, and he would carry that love afar in his travels, as Paul had done.

His love of God had been forged by suffering and sacrifice behind the Iron Curtain. His devotion to the Church, to our Lord, and to Mary had been tested by enemies. The world was ready for a Pope from the Third World who immediately extended his arms in love, and then folded them across his chest in sacrifice, all within the first minutes of the new pontificate.

It was evening when the Pope turned from the balcony and the great doors closed behind him.

But it was a new day for the Church.

May Jesus Christ be praised. Dearest brothers and sisters, we are still grieved after the death of our most beloved Pope John Paul I. And now the most eminent Cardinals have called a new Bishop of Rome. They have called him from a distant country, distant but always so close through the communion in the Christian faith and tradition. I was afraid to accept this nomination, but I did it in the spirit of obedience to our Lord Jesus Christ and of total confidence in His Mother, the most holy Madonna.

I do not know whether I can explain myself well in your...our Italian language. If I make a mistake, you will correct me. And so I present myself to you all to confess our common faith, our hope, our confidence in the Mother of Christ and of the Church, and also to start anew on this road of history and of the Church, with the help of God and with the help of men.

Pope John Paul II
October 16, 1978

2 The Man in the Pope

While the election of John Paul II was surprising, God had prepared the groundwork for it. In other words, there is a human explanation. His whole life was ordered to this great event. Karol Wojtyla's personal life originated from humble circumstances. There was the framework of intense sacrifice and the background of wartime in a land which had suffered greatly for the Faith. This would distinguish him from all other Popes. (The Pope and I have a spiritual affinity—we were born in the same year, 1920, three months apart. Also, our mothers had the same name, Amelia.)

From his earliest years, he was not marked to be a priest. He had been well-educated in Polish culture as widely as possible. He had the marvelous academic formation of the classics and the history of his great country at least until Hitler's over-throw. His personal life has known sorrow, his mother having died when he was nine years old, his sister and brother also having died young. I have read that it was actually after a long time of prayer, kneeling by his father in death, that he seems to have resolved to be a priest. From that moment, it was decided, as far as he was concerned. He was 21 years old.

The years of his youth and his academic interests ultimately strengthened his religious convictions. He worked in a quarry, then at a full time job in the Solvay Chemical Works once the war broke out. What Pope of modern times came from such an austere Third World background? Then, to have been an active supporter of the anti-Nazi resistance and to have studied in an underground seminary; what an unusual prelude to the papacy.

Unlike his predecessors in the See of Krakow, he was not of noble blood, yet the unforgettable nobleman Cardinal Sapieha of Krakow saw something in the young Wojtyla which would make him a man of destiny. The Cardinal received the young student Wojtyla into his episcopal residence where he supervised his seminary training. Many years later, Cardinal Wojtyla would return, to live in that very house in which he had once studied secretly.

The new Cardinal Wojtyla had experienced suffering, war, privation and sacrifice firsthand. He had dealt successfully with the enemies of God and of the Church.

Paraphrasing his own words, love had grown within him in its own fashion. In his heart there beat the pulse of mankind. What had begun within him as a boy would not be destroyed. He knew the difference between right and wrong.

This "love growing within" is not found often among those of us who grew up in an era of permissiveness, if not apathy. It prevented his growing bitter which he might easily have become in view of the times.

It was not surprising when at the talk he gave in the Yankee Stadium on October 2, 1979, the Holy Father citing the biblical account of Lazarus and Dives asked us to share with the less fortunate of the world. He could do so without hesitancy. He had practiced what he preached. He had studied in that school. He was not ashamed of the privilege of doing without, which he had personally experienced. "The task is immense and it is an enthralling one." Pope John Paul II invited us to a simple way of living, a lifestyle that is unselfish. This is the man we have as Pope.

The life-style of many of the members of
our rich and permissive societies is easy,
and so is the life-style of increasing
groups inside the poorer countries....
Christians will want to be in the van-
guard in favoring ways of life that
decisively break with the frenzy of
consumerism, exhausting and joyless....
We must find a simple way of being.

Pope John Paul II
Yankee Stadium
October 2, 1979

3 The Priest in the Pope

Just imagine being a pastor and being sent a future Pope as your assistant! This is what happened in 1948 when Karol Wojtyla returned from Rome to begin his first pastoral assignment in a small town in his native diocese of Krakow.

Actually, the Pope was ordained on All Saints Day, 1946. Then knowing his talents, the Cardinal sent him to the center of Thomistic Study, the Angelicum in Rome, where he met Reginald Garrigou-Lagrange who formed his theological competence. The future Pope explored the mysticism of St. John of the Cross for his doctoral dissertation. Coincidental that the Saint had likewise suffered for the Faith! Further coincidence that at this period in his life, Karol Wojtyla also met a future Pope, Paul VI, who was assigned as his mentor.

The striking thing is that this young priest who was part of a "gens lucifuga" in Poland is in Rome allowed to have these influences open to him, to form his priesthood.

This encouraged the young priest who would, upon his return to Poland, combine his parish work with teaching at the University of Krakow and with his own studies leading to a second doctorate in Theology at the State University of Krakow, a formidable challenge.

His early priesthood contributed much, as might be expected, to the happiness of the young Father Wojtyla. This is the period of his life with which so many other priests can identify—the years spent with the young when you are young, sharing their dreams and ideals. The Pope learned from the young, and he became their mentor on skiing trips, canoeing, camping in the beautiful mountains and lakes which he loved so well. What inspiration to our young priests today to be the companion of joy and the example of friendship! Some of the Pope's former students remained his friends, and some eventually accompanied him to Rome for his installation. Their old friend had become Pope!

When only twelve years a priest, in 1958, Father Wojtyla was made Auxiliary Bishop of Krakow and six years later became Archbishop of that See. How interesting that he would succeed to the royal Cathedral of the Wowel in Krakow where once he had gone as a young man during Holy Week to be enthralled as the unforgettable Cardinal Sapieha presided at Tenebrae and the Holy Week Liturgy.

Later, Cardinal Wyszinski, the Primate of Poland who had suffered imprisonment under the Nazis, and Cardinal Wojtyla, the junior Cardinal, were both prominent at Vatican II. The former was one of the twelve presiding officers, and the latter gave at least two very scholarly presentations and became very well known among his fellow bishops. This, no doubt, prompted invitations from all over the world. In America he was invited to lecture at Harvard and Princeton. He became well known by many of his compatriots in America.

Looking in retrospect at the priesthood of the future Pope, we can see a tapestry woven by God. When he visited the United States in October, 1979, the people were captivated by the "priest" in the Pope and the fibers that composed his priesthood. They looked beyond his person to his priesthood, charitable and warm yet founded on justice and truth over many years. This priest would move forward the saving work of the Christ.

Pope John Paul II the priest is going to have a surprising effect on priestly vocations throughout the world. I understand that the number of vocations in Poland has increased greatly just since the papal visit. The Pope loves priests, and he is preserving the priesthood in its generous response to the call of our Lord. How can the response change from yes to no? His own priesthood, laboriously shaped, is inspiration for us all. The process of that priesthood and his concern for that process is described in the warm passage that follows.

It is important that one's commitment be made with full awareness and personal freedom. Consider whether Christ is calling you to the celibate life. You can make a responsible decision for celibacy only after you have reached the firm conviction that Christ is indeed offering you this gift, which is intended for the good of the Church and for the service of others.

Perseverance in fidelity is a proof, not of human strength and courage but of the efficacy of God's grace.

Develop an ever greater hunger for the Word of God. Meditate on this Word daily and study it continually, so that your whole life may become a proclamation of Christ, the Word made flesh. In this Word of God are the beginning and end of all ministry.

Pope John Paul II
Philadelphia

One of the seminarians who had exchanged a white zucchetto for the one the Holy Father had on, could think of only this to say, "Holy Father, we love you very much." To which the Holy Father responded for all to hear, "Ah, not as much as I love you."

4 The Priest Forever

A French journalist called him "le cure du monde," the world's parish priest. That is how we priests see John Paul II. It seems to be what he wants us to see him as, what he truly is, "a parish priest." A parish priest is close to people. But more importantly, from this consideration, he is regarded by the people as "priest," their priest. If ever you "feel" the priesthood, it is as a parish priest. You feel the need for priesthood, the regard for it, the simple yet profound dignity of it. Then you know why you have been called by God—namely, to serve the people. In that service, your life is exalted.

In the Philadelphia visit, the Holy Father spoke of that priesthood. He said the priesthood is forever—this parish priest of the world. He upheld the teaching of the Church and explained the plan of God. He knows the needs of the people for permanency and for stability in the priesthood. He has seen people cry when that permanency is deserted by those to whom they have opened their hearts in confidence to confess their sins. The Pope completely understands the complexities of human nature, but he has also lived through the dourest of decades marked by a mania of departures.

The Pope left no doubt that he is not sympathetic toward the renunciation of the vows by priests. "Priesthood is forever. We do not return the gift once given. It cannot be that God who gave the impulse to say 'yes,' now wishes to hear 'no.'" He said: "It is 'deeply fitting,' that priests should remain celibate after the example of our Lord, Jesus Christ."

The Pope asked "all the faithful of the Church in the United States to pray for priests so that each and every one of them will repeatedly say 'yes' to the call he has received, remain constant in preaching the Gospel message, and be faithful forever as the companion of our Lord Jesus Christ."

This plea is based on the institution of Christ. It is as Christ wanted it to be, and forever. The Church has faithfully maintained this—this was the explanation of the Pope.

Is it any wonder that during the American visit, as the papal entourage processed, the people waved banners and papal flags and sang endlessly "Sto lat," a joyful Polish song often sung at birthdays and celebrations? Translated from the Polish, the song's title means "May you live 100 years." They want that for the Pope. They want it for the priest, as Christ wanted it.

You get to realize this when you are among the people—you are their priest; they won't let you go; you are caught up in that desire they have for permanency for their priest, especially if you are truly in their midst. They are an undertow; they sweep you along.

This is how Pope John Paul II feels about priesthood, and he is as much a priest as possible.

During the time I was a worker, the deepest questions of my life became crystal-
lized: my humanistic, Polonistic, artistic
and literary interests...all of that in some
way boiled up in my soul and resulted in
the priestly calling.

John Paul II

5 The Source of the Pope's Strength

The surprise, though no surprise, source of the Pope's strength is our Lord present in the Eucharist.

I have read in one of the biographies that the very best representation of the Pope is of him kneeling humbly in prayer before the Blessed Sacrament. I think of the Pope most often in this way, kneeling and praying with his head on the shoulder of the Eucharistic Christ.

This is the way the Pope prays. Can we do otherwise? He emphasizes for us that adoration, petition, thanksgiving, and reparation before the Blessed Sacrament are the best way to Jesus. He refers in his sermons to "our Eucharistic Jesus" and becomes most eloquent when he seems to find in the Eucharist "a God who breathes, lives and acts" (Claudel).

I was particularly impressed that when the Pope entered the cathedrals in Boston, New York and Chicago and the National Shrine of the Immaculate Conception in Washington, he would kneel before the altar of the Eucharist, frequently holding his head in his hands in quiet recollection. We all prayed with him for the success of the journey of faith.

The Pope is obviously a very active man, an activist who loves people and is definitely sociable. But the success of that activity lies in long hours of prayer. The soul of the apostolate is Eucharistic prayer. Social action is necessary but useless unless preceded by prayerful recollection. The vertical must precede the horizontal.

So near is God and yet so far for those who have forgotten the importance of Eucharistic adoration. Are not the cloisters of our contemplatives the power houses of success in the apostolate? How foolhardy we were to disconnect the source, to effect a spiritual energy crisis!

Each night the Pope kneels at his prie-dieu and prays for us in the presence of the Eucharistic God. The prodigal son will get new courage to lay his head on the shoulder of the Father. The whole Church will take strength from this essential prayer, much in the same manner that the Italians were heartened as the Pope carried the Blessed Sacrament through the streets of Rome in the Corpus Christi procession in 1979—for the first time in ten years. The Pope was telling us not only to see God first and foremost, but to cling strongly to His presence in mind and heart.

The high point of each station of the Pope's pilgrimage in America was the Mass celebrated in the presence of thousands. The Pope reminds us that the Church's principal means of sustenance is the action of the Eucharist. It combines sacrifice and the constant presence of the Savior. The Pope has helped us to find Jesus. He refers to the Eucharistic Sacrifice as an "audience with Jesus." From that audience we depart with the strength that our Lady and the disciples had when they came down from Calvary.

Love Jesus present in the Eucharist. He is present in a sacrificial way in Holy Mass which renews the sacrifice of the cross. To go to Mass means going to Calvary to meet Him, our Redeemer.

He comes to us in Holy Communion and remains present in the tabernacles of our churches, for He is our friend. He is everyone's friend...on our way through life; we need confidence and friendship so much.

Pope John Paul II
November 6, 1978

SECTION TWO

God Will Strike a Giant Bell

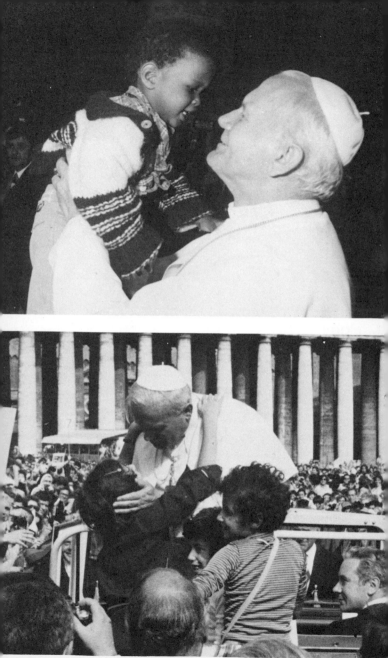

6 The Personal Secret Revealed

The personality of the Holy Father radiates his spirituality in an exceptionally descriptive way. He is an active-contemplative. He loves mingling in crowds; he loves taking children into his arms, lifting them into the air; he is utterly unpredictable in that he will delay and talk to this person or that child. He was intrigued by the hard hats in New York as Cardinal Cooke pointed up to them high in the buildings, perched like birds on the limbs of trees. His tendency is to be sociable. Yet with all this he has a profoundly serious side reminiscent of St. John of the Cross, of whom he is a disciple. His writings, the poetry especially, are quite definitely in the area of contemplation. They reflect his educational background and even more so his background of childhood austerity. At the Angelicum, under the supervision of Father

Reginald Garrigou-Lagrange, he wrote "The Concept of Faith in St. John of the Cross," and that influence is never absent from his personality, his spirituality, or his writings.

I was intrigued by the following which he wrote as a young priest while in Rome: "The system under which I am learning is not only tremendously wise, it is also beautiful. And at the same time it speaks with such simplicity. It turns out that thought and depth never need many words. Perhaps the deeper the thought, the less it needs words." This philosophical attitude is his personality. It pervades his writing most conspicuously in his poetry. Evolving, therefore, is a fascinating linking of study, spirituality, personality, and writing, though not necessarily in that order.

St. John of the Cross, as those know so well who have studied the mystic, wrote of the "dark night of the soul." This indicates a suffering that some must pass through who would find God. Certainly Pope John Paul II has experienced in his personal life a dark night of the soul in his opposition to the enemies of the Church. It troubled him that some would make Poland appear as an atheistic country.

Frequently in *Sign of Contradiction*, the book that is the published version of the magnificent retreat which Cardinal Wojtyla gave in 1976 to the Roman Curia at the invitation of Pope Paul VI, he quotes St. John of the Cross concerning the mystery of the interior life, saying "man needs mystery." His Carmelite devotion to contemplation has never left him; it has formed his spirituality as well as his personality. Hence, he becomes for the Church a combination of Western spirituality and Eastern mysticism, a key to his personal magnetism.

He loves to delve introspectively into the mystery of God and man, yet he also says "to travel is to live"—perhaps this is always the propensity for philosophy and theology. *The Acting Person*, which was published in 1969, is his philosophical treatise. In 1979, it was published in an enlarged edition in English. It is regarded as a deep experience into the probing of man as a person. Cardinal Wojtyla is always "wondering."

I find it very interesting that much of the Holy Father's life is found in his poetry and prose. In *Easter Vigil and Other Poems*, which I have read with great profit and pleasure, so much of "him" is found. Of course he writes of his great favorite, the Blessed Mother, but also of "The Car Factory Worker." He tells of the secretary at her typewriter. Then, in "A Bishop's Thoughts on Giving the Sacrament of Confirmation in a Mountain Village," we see his life almost in panorama. I think he has not written much poetry since becoming Cardinal. He loves to write; there's no doubt of that. It was an outlet for so much of his personality, so much of his priesthood. I hope he will find time to write as Pope. The fascination of the Pope is particularly evident in this literary area. Here one obviously comes to know him, because it is a camera which photographs his many facets.

I love the poem about the Pope by Julius Slowacki, famous Polish poet of the last century. The poem was written in 1848, perhaps prophetically written about Pope John Paul II, calling him a beacon to God's realm. It follows:

In the middle of all their quarrels,
God will strike a giant bell
For a Slavonic Pope.
This one will not shrink from critics like the
    others:
Fearless as Christ, He will face all coura-
    geously.
His world—just a mire!

His countenance a radiating lamp for
    service,
And mankind will follow this beacon to
    God's realm.
To his prayers, not only the people, but the
    others will listen:
This charism—a miracle!

He is already approaching, the dispenser of
    a new global force:
His words will cause a pause and reflection,
As a stream of divine light floods all hearts.
His understanding and wisdom are of the
    SPIRIT:
The energy needed to raise up the Lord's
    world.

And so, comes the Slavonic Pope, all
    people's brother
Who will bring vitality and rebirth to all.
A choir of angels adorn with graces the
    THRONE.
For he will teach love, and not as other
    leaders reach for arms.

His sacramental strength will emanate to
    the world:
The DOVE will guide his words and actions
To bring the good news of the SPIRIT'S
    presence.
Heaven will open in complete accord
Because he stands and unites the world to
    the THRONE.

Humanity will embrace in brotherhood to
    his call,
And the SPIRIT will reach out to the
    farthest ends.
A solemn dignity of this spirit will be visi-
    ble:
Such a One, you will see soon—a shadow,
    then the face.

He will purge all decay, pretense, revolt and
    sham:
He will dispel all ills and ventilate interiors
    of churches,
And even brighten and renew entries.
He will bring health, charity, truth and
    salvation to earth.
God will shine as the dawn in all creation.

Julius Slowacki, 1848

The two vocations, the priest's
and the poet's, coexist and act on
each other in the same person.

Julius Slowacki

7 The Pope of the Outdoors

One of the poignant moments after John Paul II became Pope was when the Polish people serenaded him with a native song saying how much he would miss the mountains of Poland and the happy times he had spent there climbing and skiing and singing in the company of his beloved student friends.

This is a warm side of the Pope with which we should identify. We priests should lead others to the appreciation of the outside world, the creation of a very good God. It is a beautiful world, and the Pope inhales its beauty. He has traveled widely and misses none of the wealth of the creation. Especially does he love the landscape of Poland and its mountainous regions, although his birthplace is in the foothills.

They say that as a young priest and even when he was a Cardinal, he walked in the mountains. He rode a bike in the High Taru mountains. Of course, we all know his now famous quip spoken in Italy in which he said that as much as 50% of the Polish Cardinals ski, referring to himself, counting the only other Polish Cardinal, the Primate Cardinal Wyszynski, as the other 50%. We have seen him now as Pope being presented with a pair of skis, and he is looking up at the skis admiringly. I have never skied and, secretly, I don't want the Pope to ski anymore lest some accident befall him. Yet to those who do ski, I guess it's as easy as walking. When he was a student in Rome during winter time he also engaged in the winter sports.

They say his installation as Pope was arranged to take place in the morning out of consideration for the Italians who were to participate in the soccer match which was scheduled for that afternoon. His heart is in the outdoors.

While an avid student, the young Wojtyla was always interested in and very good at sports. As a priest he combined this with his pastoral ministry to the youth of his parishes and at the University. Many of these excursions in the outdoors allowed him contact with students at the very time when the Communists were restricting any youth apostolates.

I can imagine how he enjoyed giving conferences to those young people who were being denied a formal religious practice. It was this type of activity that never allowed the complete Communist takeover in Poland. He offered Mass outdoors many times, and all these events allowed a personal friendship with a priest who was loved, revered, admired and ultimately followed even to Rome.

At the age of 38, when he was named Auxiliary Bishop of Krakow, they had all they could do to locate him since he was off with young students on a holiday canoeing trip. After the notification, he asked if he could resume his holiday.

This, of course, makes the Pope wonderfully human and identifiable with the many Americans who are sports-minded.

This makes him very understandable, and somehow, it seems to me, this will result in an increase of priestly vocations. I earnestly hope so. There is a special appeai in a Pope who loves the outdoors and the challenge it brings to the adventure-minded.

I thank my young friends.... They brought me
closer to nature with them; I began practicing
mountain climbing, skiing, canoeing, bicycling.

John Paul II

8 Be My Friend

Certainly it is clear that we have a friendly Pope. It isn't simply that he smiles a great deal; it is just that he radiates happiness. Sometimes his eyes even have a twinkle.

This is certainly evident when he twirls children over his head or lifts them up to kiss them lovingly. So also when he puts on the Mexican sombrero to the enjoyment of all. He enjoyed the young people at the Madison Square Garden Youth Rally, joining in with them in the now famous "woo-woo." Of course, this is a happy human side that we have not seen in Popes. I think it stems from his Polish origin, for who is happier than a group of Poles doing their native Polkas? This helps to make Pope John Paul II the people's Pope. He seems to engender a sense of celebration among people. When he visited Harvard University in 1976, he gave a serious lecture, but, the friendliness came through. His host said: "He is one of the most impressive men I've ever met in my whole life. He has an absolutely radiant personality." That radiance is an inner happiness, an attunement to God's will. It overflows in his desire to join in with singing groups. This is John Paul's spirit of faith, joyful faith, positive Catholicism.

A Polish-American priest, whom I know well, told me recently that he met the Holy Father in Doylestown, Pennsylvania, and the Holy Father, bidding him goodbye, held my friend's arm and said in Polish, "Be my friend!" He seems to be saying that to everyone whom he meets. It is the happiness that he radiates, and it is addressed to the dignity of each human person.

He has told us, "You are the friends and companions of the Pope. Do not deny me the joy of watching you study and play responsibly!" This informality marks him as the first Pope whom we have seen allowing himself this ease. We saw it in the early moments of his pontificate, when after his Mass of Installation, the people remained under his audience window for a long time. He told them finally that they must go home and eat, and so must the Pope have his lunch. In Chicago, to a similar group, he tilted his head, holding his hands to one ear, indicating sleep and said, "Go to sleep, go to sleep." He has provoked laughter on

another occasion by saying jokingly, "finally we can all go home and have dinner."
This relaxed manner is not part of a sce-
nario, it is a carry over from his Polish personality, a certain "joie de vivre." I don't
know how to say that expression in Polish
or I would.

This happiness has conquered the media; it established instant contact with the
press. It put them in a comfortable attitude.
One American reporter wrote that the Pope
told him to "write well" about him—with a
mischievous grin.

The Holy Father regards the papacy as
an opportunity for kindness and service
and dedication. This will prompt the Pope
to lead the Church with hope and not facile
optimism and to give a new vitality joyfully
to the Church as it goes toward the year
2,000.

God has given him a mission not given
to anyone else, as Cardinal Newman says,
and the Pope is aware of that. He feels
destined, serenely courageously so.

There is a multitude of anecdotal
stories that brightly illustrate the humor-
ous, joyful, friendly spirit of this very
contemplative Pope. It is not necessary to
document further that this Pope, like Jesus
Christ, is saying to us, "I no longer call you
servants but friends." "Be my friend."

I wish to assure all Americans—
Catholics, Protestants and Jews,
people of all churches, and all men
and women of good will—of my friendship,
respect and esteem.

John Paul II

9 He Speaks Our Language

John Paul II is a forceful public speaker. Much of his ability as orator is native talent—he has a strong voice and a very pleasant quality of tone. However, there is no doubt that his great liking for acting as a young man helped him to develop projection. He had seriously thought of the classical and professional stage and belonged to a distinguished group of performers in his college days. This gave him a stage presence and an audience rapport.

The Polish people knew this for years. They were well aware of his speaking talents and that he loved to preach. He also was invited to lecture in other countries, because his reputation as a speaker grew widely. His lecture at Harvard was so popularly acclaimed that someone at that time mentioned him as a papal possibility. Not the least factor in this popularity is his unique facility with language. On New Year's Day, 1980, he gave greetings in 34 languages.

This ability was evident at the balcony scene when he first addressed the world as Pope. His Italian was clear and firm and his voice was strong. It was evident that this Pope would be at home in any language. He has had a proficiency in language since he was a young student and he seems to like to play with words. Remember when he said on that October 16th day, "our" Italian language? Also when he asked the Italians "to correct me if I am wrong"?

I think what most amazes us Americans is how well the Pope speaks our language. In the many talks he gave here, it was only "skyscraper" at Shea stadium that gave him slight difficulty and he quickly corrected that. For a person so fluent in French and Italian as he is, the accent or the emphasis is certainly a puzzlement in English. Yet the Pope was amazingly faultless. Of course, his subject matter was so serious and at times ponderous, that he obviously did not want to falter or to speak in a non-intelligible foreign accent. It must have been difficult at the United Nations, coming face to face with delegates from all over the world; to speak so fluently in English. It has endeared him to us, as well as to the many people he has addressed in their native tongue. It has definitely "epiphanized" the Church, making it an effective light of all nations.

A young friend of mine who is a convert to our faith said, "It seemed good to have the Pope speaking English—I felt close to him." I thought much about that remark as the Pope went from one American city to the other, speaking slowly and somewhat ponderously, but never without the desired personal effect. It was an awesome undertaking to relate to the inhabitants of each city, and he succeeded admirably. What a beautiful week it was, to find so much positive inspiration from the Pope! It was like someone cheering us on from the sidelines. He was someone who knew the game and understood the plays and the players.

Stemming from his acting days, he has mastered the effective pause, and he frequently punctuates his talks with that pause. This is a good technique for any speaker, establishing necessary suspense more than once in the progression of a particular train of thought.

His voice, his linguistic arts, and his forensic ability combine to make this Pope a surprise to the world, a very "understandable" surprise for me. His hand is on the pulse of the world because he speaks the many languages of mankind. Because of this, I feel the Church will never be the same.

I prefer speaking impromptu.
I feel then my brain works.

John Paul II

SECTION THREE

The Heart of the Pope

10 Heart Speaks to Heart

The Pope has shown to the world a tremendous capacity for friendship and brotherly love. He has not concealed his emotions in this regard. In fact, he said that the Polish heart in particular "is not sufficient to contain such an emotion." His leave-taking from the Polish people, from his sons in the priesthood, so many of whom were ordained through his episcopal ministry, was tender and warm. His departure from his episcopal see of Krakow was deeply felt by him. The Holy Father has taught this lesson to us in an emotionless, cold time when the bonds that unite the family of man are so fragile and so easily severed.

The Holy Father has said "it is difficult to think and speak without a very deep emotion" of the trying recent times that the Church in Poland has endured. Yet he is proud that because of this suffering, the Church in Poland "has acquired a special significance in the context of the universal Church." The Church in Poland has become an object of great interest as a result; "it has become the Church of a special testimony to which the whole world looks." This circumstance lent to an even deeper emotional parting on his part.

It flowed over to the very touching leave-taking that the whole world witnessed as Cardinal Primate Wyszynski paid his personal homage. The Pope rose to greet him and held him in a strong embrace resting the Primate's head upon his shoulder. The words he said to the Primate are more than friendship, more than brotherly love, more than affection or emotion. They have the ring of poetry:

"Venerable and beloved Cardinal Primate, allow me to tell you just what I think. This Polish Pope, who today, full of fear of God, but also of trust, is beginning a new pontificate, but would not be on Peter's chair were it not for your faith which did not retreat before prisons and suffering. Were it not for your heroic hope, your unlimited trust in the Mother of the Church! Were it not for Jasna Gora, and the whole period of the history of the Church in our country, together with your ministry as bishop and Primate!"

His heart speaks to the heart of his beloved mentor. Here the Pope openly expresses his limitless admiration for the Primate who is a symbol of hope and resistance. The Pope tenderly recalls the great devotion of Cardinal Wyszynski to our Lady. In this singularly beautiful expression of esteem, the Pope includes all the Polish people, religious and lay, with whom the Primate is one. The Pope is not chauvinistic in this but rather states a reality that "springs from the law of the human heart."

He associates the patriotism which is so much part of him with this loving renunciation. In parting, he extends his loving embrace "to these fields rich in varied flowers, silvered with wheat and gilded with rye," recalling the words of the poet Mickiewicz. The mountains and valleys, the lakes and rivers are lovingly viewed as the Pope leaves his native land and its people. All have a special claim to his emotion, affection and prayer.

O Mountaineer, do you not grieve
For the land that gave you birth,
for the forests of spruce and the
meadows and the streams of running
silver?
O Mountaineer, do you not grieve?

Polish Folk Song

His gratitude extends to all these people and places that have prepared him for the "call made to me by Christ on October 16th in the Sistine Chapel." All this accompanies him to St. Peter's Chair. "All this constitutes a layer of my soul which I cannot leave."

These various quotations from the Holy Father give a striking insight into his warm nature. It is a priceless treasure that the Pope conveys to us who have grown casual and even indifferent to our loved ones, to our beloved heritage, to our native land. It is the supreme lesson of the law of the human heart.

Conserve the land well, so that your
children's children and generations after them
will inherit an even richer land than was
entrusted to you.

It gives me great pleasure to be here today
with you in the heartland of America in this
lovely St. Patrick's Church at the Irish settle-
ment. On your farms you are close to God's
nature; in your work on the land you follow
the rhythm of the seasons and in your hearts
you feel close to each other as children of a
common Father and as brothers and sisters of
Christ.

Pope John Paul II
Des Moines

11 The Informal Pope

I have attempted to write informal essays because the subject of the essays is the first informal Pope we have ever known. We know the Italian press nicknamed him "Cyclone Wojtyla" as early as November, 1978, a month after his installation. He is spontaneous, quick, and independently decisive; they recognized that. Informality comes naturally to him. The stilted, the unnatural is quickly rejected by him, even when suggested by protocol. From the beginning, it became apparent that informality would be his style, though not interfering with his personal dignity or command. He is simply at ease with all, from the College of Cardinals to the smallest child. This informality of manner stems from his being Polish yet it has endeared him to the Italians. He has not hesitated to insert himself into their lives. When they welcome him with signs written in Polish, he says, "Is that perhaps because you think that the Pope doesn't know much Italian?"

Many of his informal actions have attracted worldwide reaction such as his consenting to perform the marriage of a young couple, the daughter of a street cleaner and one who installs burglar alarms. When the bride asked the Pope, "Can I give you a kiss?", he answered, "And why not?" We also know he baptized a baby, following a spur of the moment request. His audiences on Wednesday and his summer receptions at Castelgandolfo for the Italian and Polish youth are marked by a tremendous warmness as he moves among the young people. Song is a great part of his informal style. He strongly believes that singing brings people together in an instant communication. Entering into this means of mass communication, he has entered the lives of many young people much as he did in Poland in his camping and hiking days with the youth of the University. Yet with it all he has been known to say, "I am the Pope. I know how to behave."

The Pope may be reminding us that we have lost the simple way of life which is marked by dignity yet informality. We have become too structured, too complicated in that so many of our movements and relationships are not spontaneous. We are the victims of every "how to" book that has ever been written. We are told "how to think," "how to act," and "how to react" in every circumstance. Our lives are psychology-conscious and our motives are psychoanalyzed *ad nauseam.* Our relationships crumble because they are unnatural and coached. We are unsure of ourselves and of each other because we are not at home with even those of our household. This may be a facet of our strictly-business approach to life. It may be our deep concern with efficiency in the Madison Avenue tradition. This may have deprived our Christian relationships of the informality and spontaneity which the Pope seems determined to restore.

When a soul strains after simplicity and unity,
a combination mind and body clamors for
duplicity and diversity. Made for harmony,
man clutters up his life with complications.

Hubert Van Zeller

12 All Yours

Shepherd I made the Papal seal and the Pope's motto known to the world. The coat of arms was painted brilliantly on the side of the airplane. Of course, it was also prominently displayed throughout the visit on flags and banners of all types.

The coat of arms of Pope John Paul II is very interesting and has personally intrigued me from the first. I now have a hand carving of it as a gift from one of my parishioners. It is in our church for the devotion of all. There is a similar one placed so as to greet all who come to our home. The coat of arms is intended as an act of homage to the central mystery of our religion, the redemption.

The main representation is a cross, whose form, however, does not correspond to the customary heraldic model. The reason for the unusual placement of the vertical section of the cross is readily apparent if you consider the second object depicted on the coat of arms—a large and majestic capital letter M. This is placed under the horizontal bar of the cross recalling the presence of Mary beneath the cross and her singular participation in the redemption, the Mother of the Redeemer.

The coat of arms is a great manifestation of the beautiful and powerful devotion of the Holy Father to the Virgin Mary. Further indication of that same devotion is in his motto which the Holy Father chose when he became a bishop: "Totus tuus," which means: "All Yours." Of course, this is not any wonder since the celebrated shrine of Our Lady of Czestochowa is in the province of Krakow. It is at that shrine that the Polish people for centuries have prayed in their devotion to the Mother of God.

The Pope has very soon earned for himself the title "The Pope of Mary." Immediately upon greeting the world from the balcony of St. Peter's, in that now well-known speech delivered in Italian, he mentioned the name of Mary three times within those first few minutes: "total confidence in His Mother," "the most holy Madonna," "our confidence in the Mother of Christ." This won him both the immediate love of the Italians and of all people devoted to Mary.

No fear of a false ecumenism can discourage us now from mentioning the name of Mary and from invoking her. How discouraging were these past years which saw the abolition of devotions to Mary and sometimes the removal of her statue from our churches proper! The constant Marian devotion of the People of God was, however, never abolished.

The Pope has resumed the magnificent habit of his predecessors and recites the Angelus on Sunday together with the faithful. The Pope prays at the window of his balcony and the people pray below in the Square. (In our parish church to honor the Pope of Mary we recite the Angelus each day before the noon Mass.) The first time the Pope said the Angelus in this fashion was immediately after the solemn Mass of his inauguration.

The Pope said that this emphasis on the "history of salvation reaches its climax and, at the same time, begins again its definitive form" when the Virgin of Nazareth accepts the announcement of the angel and utters the words: "Let it be done to me according to your word" (Lk. 1:38).

I am reminded of the fact that we can offend God by honoring Mary too little; we can never offend Him by honoring Mary too much. He honored her, calling her to be the Mother of His divine Son—the greatest honor.

Paul VI had given Mary the title "Mother of the Church." He named her so in a solemn way, and we began to pray to her by that name. To lay even greater emphasis on that title, Paul VI, together with the Council Fathers, went to the major basilica of Mary, St. Mary Major, where Mary has been surrounded with love for many centuries.

Following in the footsteps of his saintly Predecessor, on December 8, 1978, John Paul II crossed that same threshold of Mary to entrust the Church to Mary, and to entrust himself to her, and "all those whom he serves."

The Pope gives a great new sign of hope —Maria spes mea—Mary, Our Hope.

Hail, O Mother, Queen of the world!
You are the Mother of fair love.
You are the Mother of Jesus, the source
of all grace,
the perfume of every virtue, the mirror
of all purity.
You are joy in weeping,
victory in battle, hope in death.
How sweet your name tastes in our mouth,
how harmoniously it rings in our ears,
what rapture it brings to our hearts!
You are the happiness of the suffering,
the crown of martyrs, the beauty of virgins.
We beg you, guide us after this exile,
to possession of your Son, Jesus. Amen.

Prayer recited by Pope John Paul II
in a Homily, May 1, 1979

SECTION FOUR

The Mind of the Pope

13 Sign of Contradiction

John Cardinal Krol of Philadelphia has stated that: "It is rare and probably unique for a Pope to have preached a spiritual retreat to one of his Predecessors." We know that Cardinal Wojtyla preached the annual Lenten retreat in March, 1976, to Pope Paul VI and his collaborators. It consisted of 22 conferences, for which, they say, the Holy Father had only a month to prepare. First he wrote them in Polish, then Italian. It now appears as the first full-length book published by the Pope. It has the title *Sign of Contradiction.* Its merits are beyond my recommendation. Everyone can find in this book the authentic Church, the loving Christ.

Its central theme is taken from the words used by Simeon (Lk. 2:34) describing Christ as a great sign of contradiction, also as a sign which arouses opposition. The Pope was immersed in that knowledge from the Polish experience, his own Catholic country having withstood the threats of Communism.

When John Paul II gave his inaugural address on October 22, 1978, he told us this same theme: "Brothers and sisters, do not be afraid to welcome Christ and to accept His power. Open wide the doors for Christ. To His power open the boundaries of states, economic and political systems, the vast fields of culture, civilization and development." The Pope places our hope in Christ, but he warns us of "a new advent—a time of expectation and also of one crucial temptation—in a word still the same temptation that we know of from the third chapter of Genesis though in one sense more deeply rooted than ever. A time of great trial but also of great hope for just such a time as this we have been given the sign: Christ, Sign of Contradiction, and the woman clothed with the sun 'a great sign in the heavens.' "

"This is not an easy book," Cardinal Hume states in the foreword to the British edition, but if read thoughtfully—well, you are listening to the Pope!

In the foreword to the Italian edition, Cardinal Wyszynski, Primate of Poland, says the golden thread that runs through the talks is the "yes" that Karol Wojtyla

has always said, together with his countrymen, to God, to the Church of Christ,
and to His Mother.

What better than to incline us to that
same generous affirmation in the face of
contradictory times! No treatment of *Sign
of Contradiction* would be complete without actual quotation. Found on page 198:
"The times in which we are living provide
particularly strong confirmation of the
truth of what Simeon said: Jesus is both the
light that shines for mankind and at the
same time a sign of contradiction. If now—
on the threshold of the last quarter-century
before the second millennium, after the
Second Vatican Council, and in the face of
the terrible experiences that the human
family has undergone and is still under-
going—Jesus Christ is once again revealing
Himself to men as the light of the world, has
He not also become at one and the same
time that sign which, more than ever, men
are resolved to oppose?"

This theme seems to form the spiritual
basis of the Holy Father, hope in Christ yet
suffering for Christ.

The book reflects the theology, philosophy and the literary range of the Holy
Father which enabled him to make his
mark in the Church from the time he was a
young priest at the Angelicum. It enabled
him to combine his pastoral ministry in

Poland with an international reputation as a lecturer. It enabled him to write numerous books and articles for scholarly magazines.

It now is no wonder; it becomes clear why Pope Paul VI invited him to probe the *Sign of Contradiction*. Is he to be that sign in the papacy?

Sign of Contradiction reflects the deep faith and spirituality of the Pope expressed with Gospel simplicity and clarity. It expresses sound scriptural doctrine and profound spirituality. It can serve as a blueprint for a truly active Christian life.

John Cardinal Krol
Archbishop of Philadelphia

14 Praised Be Jesus Christ!

I have grown to love the first prayer with which the new Pope greeted the world: "Praised be Jesus Christ, now and forever."

It contains the complete focus of our faith—concentration on Christ and all the glory of His kingdom. It is a prayer familiar in Europe. John Paul II said it from the time he was a little boy. The Polish use it as a greeting as they pass each other on the street on their way to work or to school. Over and over again they profess their faith in Christ, casually, but with reverence, too. They live by faith. They live the faith. That was the faith that made Europe great. Christ is the center of their lives.

They love Mary, too, because she gave them Jesus. They love her as Mother of Poland.

Pope Wojtyla has been called "a man filled with Christ" by Cardinal Medeiros of Boston. That is why he said "yes" when Christ asked him what he had asked Peter two thousand years ago, "Do you love me more than these?" "Yes, I do love You— humbly, sincerely, courageously. I will be the 265th Pope." Like the Apostle whose name he took, namely Paul, "I can do all things in Him who strengthens me." Christ is his strength. He doesn't seem worried unduly about security even on his perilous journeys because, as he says, "I am in the hands of God." We should have that faith in Jesus, that real abandonment!

It was very striking, when at the Mass he said to open his pontificate, his voice rang out, "Thou art the Christ, the Son of the living God." It was as if he were saying to us, "The Church is the work of God. It is God's gift to us." God must love us if He gave us the Church and made it the extension of Himself, the enduring voice of Christ in the world. That is what makes us so worthy in God's eyes. That is why Pope John Paul II concentrates so much on man's dignity as a person. "Who do men say that I am?" It matters! "You are the Christ, the Son of the living God."

What John Paul II has done is to direct us in clear terms to the focal point of Christ. "My brothers and sisters, be not afraid to

welcome Christ and to accept Him."..."Do
not be afraid! Open up rather, open wide
the doors to Christ. Christ knows what is in
man. He alone knows." The Pope knows
how afraid we are to risk all for the Lord.
The Pope tries so hard to bring Christ and
man close to each other—the Redeemer
and the redeemed. So great is God. So great
man.

It would be wonderful if we, like the
Pope, could radiate Christ. As Cardinal
Newman says, they would see "not me but
only Jesus." This centrality of Christ por-
trays the essential work of the Catholic
Church, as I see it. Look to Christ in the
Eucharist! Find Him there! Look to Christ
in the teachings of the Church! Look to
Christ in the operation of grace! Today, we
have become involved in religious practices
which may be helpful, but they are disturb-
ingly intertwined with a certain sociability
with our fellow men. Perhaps this brings us
to Christ, but is it to the Christ of revelation
or the Christ of our own invention? I hope
the former. "Praised be Jesus Christ!"
What do we think of this Christ?

What is the Christ of revelation like?
Cardinal Medeiros of Boston has said elo-
quently, "We thank God for the gift of Pope
John Paul II to His Church; we also publicly
thank our supreme Shepherd for accepting
the sweet burden of Christ." Cardinal
Medeiros describes Christ as being con-

nected with a sweet burden. He calls it sweet but also a burden. I think what the Cardinal and the Pope mean to say is that we cannot take Christ down from the cross. Accept the whole Christ, the Sign of Contradiction.

I think that this is what John Paul II meant us to pray when he said his first words to us as Pope, "Praised be Jesus Christ, now and forever."

Dear young people:

Soon you will be making decisions that will affect the whole course of your life. If these decisions reflect Christ's attitude, then your education will be a success.

When you wonder about the mystery of yourself, look to Christ who gives you the meaning of life. When you wonder what it means to be a mature person, look to Christ who is the fullness of humanity.

Because actions speak louder than words, you are called to proclaim by the conduct of your daily lives that you really do believe that Jesus Christ is Lord.

Pope John Paul II
Madison Square Garden
October 3, 1979

15 Taking an Important Stand

When we become priests, it is to be forever. In the last twenty years, what Paul VI called "the mania" of departures set in. An estimated 2,000 laicizations a year were granted. At one point in the early 70's there were 88 departures per 1,000 priests. There was much sadness on the part of priests as they watched their brothers in the priesthood depart, much loss of morale in seminaries, a great decline in vocations to the point of crisis. The latter became the number one problem in the Church. The people became very confused, disheartened, and disenchanted.

Before John Paul II became Pope, a trend of reversal was at least on the horizon, in that the departures leveled off. The requests for laicization centered around celibacy and psychological problems. To those statistical considerations, there were many emotional overtones that are too intangible to be recorded here.

After the election of the Polish Pope, the processing of cases of laicization came to an abrupt halt. The new Pope was disturbed, and was reconsidering the situation. He was worried about the question of morale among the priests who remained in the ministry and about the morale of seminarians. It was within his right as Pope to grant this gift of dispensation or not. It was not a right to which the individual priest had claim. The Pope knew the difficulties. "You will meet difficulties. Do you think perhaps that I do not know about them? I am telling you that love overcomes all difficulties."

It was an issue that had to be tackled; it was a challenge that had to be met. There was much tension and a growing number of requests to leave was to be expected. What about doing away altogether with the requirement of celibacy in the Western Church? Or what about making it optional?

The Pope once again has spoken with characteristic firmness "for the sake of the Kingdom." He has said "no" to those favoring married priests, and he has let it be known that there will be no light dispensation of anyone from priestly vows. This matter needed such an approach—for assurance, for hope, for the sake of the Church, "for the sake of the Kingdom."

The Pope discussed all the reasons for his decision with lucidity, and he has issued many written commentaries concerning that decision, frequently calling on his own experience.

In diverse ways the Pope has encouraged us priests and the bishops to exert "every possible effort" to encourage vocations by going out in every possible way to the young people. This is the underlying reason for our writing a previously published book *This Priest Is Thankful* (St. Paul Editions, Daughters of St. Paul, 1979). It is an affirmation of the priesthood in the hope of encouraging vocations among the young.

The decision of the Pope, no doubt, will not be popular among some. The Pope is not concerned about popularity. He has done what he feels must be done. It will effect a renewed appreciation of the priestly image, resulting in an increase in vocations.

It is very easy to let oneself be guided by appearances and fall victim to a fundamental illusion in what is essential. Those who call for the secularization of priestly life and applaud its various manifestations will undoubtedly abandon us when we succumb to temptation. We shall then cease to be necessary and popular. Our time is characterized by different forms of "manipulation" and "exploitation" of man, but we cannot give in to any of these. In practical terms, the only priest who will always prove necessary to people is the priest who is conscious of the full meaning of his priesthood: the priest who believes profoundly, who professes his faith with courage, who prays fervently, who teaches with deep conviction, who serves, who puts into practice in his own life the program of the beatitudes, who knows how to love disinterestedly, who is close to everyone, and especially to those who are most in need.

Pope John Paul II
April 9, 1979

16 The Right to Life

If there is one thing that has claimed the Pope's first attention, it is the right to life. This is based on his regard for the dignity of the human person which is so much part of his very being. This has pleased many people who have long felt that the Church has not spoken out enough against the sin of abortion which has claimed 1.3 million lives in the United States each year. In our country, it is legal to abort a child even in the third trimester of pregnancy. The Supreme Court's decision to legalize abortion continues to be a chief political-religious antagonism.

As early as New Year's Eve, 1979, the Holy Father spoke at the Jesuit Church of the Gesù in Rome about the right of the unborn. That was attacked immediately by the pro-abortionists in Italy. The Pope in mid-January rejected their contention that it was an issue on which he had no right to speak. He called it a moral question pertaining to conscience in which area he had the duty to inform of the divine truth.

He called the right to life "the primordial presupposition of every other human right." He thanked those engaged in health care for following the dictates of right conscience and for resisting pressures to perform actions offensive to the sacred values of human life.

He said that the principle of divorce and the principle of abortion do not serve the construction of a better society.

"The affirmation of the value of the new life must be respected from the first moment of conception. The Church cannot dispense itself from the obligation of protecting these fundamental values."

Cardinal Benelli of Florence reiterated the position of the Italian hierarchy against abortion also on New Year's Day, 1979, citing that "in less than five years we will have killed legally in Italy as many lives as were exterminated in World War I if the legal abortion rate continues at its present rate." The pro-abortionists then demonstrated outside the house of Cardinal Benelli.

All these things have not prevented the Pope from repeatedly stressing the abortion issue throughout his audiences and travels. Pro-life groups are now heartened at gains being made in the Congress and their political influence is on the upswing in a long battle ahead. Demonstrations in Washington on January 22nd, the anniversary of the Supreme Court decision, continue to decry the official figure of 1.3 million lives a year aborted.

The Holy Father is going to support the pro-life groups throughout the world by what he says publicly and does in behalf of the unborn—and that, until the battle is won. He will continue to defend the fundamental values with serene courage.

The test of a relationship is not the agony of parting or the joy of meeting again after separation. The test lies in what trouble two people are prepared to take, what sacrifices two people are prepared to make, for one another.

Hubert Van Zeller

17 The Central Commitment of the Pope

In the first year of his pontificate, six months into it, March 15, 1979, Pope John Paul II wrote his encyclical, *Redemptor hominis*—the "Redeemer of Man." It seems as though this is an accumulation, arranged in orderly manner, of all the thoughts that have been pressing upon his mind all through his life. Now that Christ has called him to his new ministry he feels bound to make these convictions universally known. The letter is clearly his own work, first written by him in Polish and then translated into the various languages for distribution. The language of it is, above all, marked by clarity and charity, hallmarks of John Paul's style. Briefly it treats Christ the Redeemer and man the redeemed. It is 24,000 words, and it focuses on the supreme dignity of man. This is the crux of the new pontificate, namely, the relationship between redemption and human dignity. The Pope calls it the "central commitment of my new ecclesial services." The single purpose of the Church is "that every man must be able to find Christ." What could be clearer?

Many subjects are covered. One of my personal favorite encyclicals of Pope Paul VI was his very first one *Ecclesiam suam*—"His Church." This first letter of John Paul II makes immediate reference to it in that the new Pope thinks the Church is internally stronger because of the pontificate of Paul VI. Though he admits that we are not free of all internal tensions, he feels that now we are better able to meet the excesses of the self-criticism of the 70's. Now we are more mature in our spirit.

The Pope dwells on the fact that technological gain may not mean spiritual advance. Has it rendered us more ready to help all, especially the needy and the weak?

The letter states a theme that the Pope reiterated in New York City at the Yankee Stadium: are the rich ready to share or have we become the slaves of things, of economic systems?

The final chapter, "The Church's Mission and Man's Destiny," calls theologians "the servants of divine truth" and stresses the need for them to remain united with the Pope and the bishops in presenting the teachings of the Church. I think the people are tired of the divisive, irresponsible forces among us. We are aware of pluralism in method, but we also are aware of the necessity for unity in the teaching of faith and morals. This explains some of the future actions that the Pope feels are necessary to preserve the sacred deposit of God's revelation, this divine truth, in union with the Magisterium.

Very interesting to me in the encyclical was the emphasis placed on the Eucharist as "center and summit of the whole sacramental life." The Pope also warns against reducing Penance merely to a celebration of community. He feels strongly about and defends the profound inward act of individual confession. This focus was badly needed.

The Pope clearly wants a period of consolidation. He wants an emphasis on the "centuries old tradition of the Church," using Vatican II as a guide, while warning Catholics not to try to out-guess the Council.

As might be expected, the encyclical closes with a prayer to the Mother of Christ whom John Paul II calls by the title conferred by Paul VI, namely, Mother of the Church.

This first encyclical told us a lot about the new Pope, about what he is thinking, about the direction in which his leadership will take us. In short, it gave redeemed man new hope from the Vicar of Christ the Redeemer.

I know that my redeemer lives.

(Job 19:25)

When a man turns his eyes to the cross, his thoughts make an abrupt about-turn. It's very strange; it's as if the one hanging on the cross, Jesus, had justified everything, it's as if at that moment—"He had justified God himself before man" (John Milton, *Paradise Lost*).

Pope John Paul II,
Sign of Contradiction
Seabury Press

18 The Pope in 2D

I have heard that in Rome they are humorously referring to the Holy Father as "The Pope in 2D." The 2D's being Doctrine and Discipline.

The Holy Father has a commitment to carry out Vatican Council II, and that Council under the action of the Holy Spirit laid emphasis on those two D's—although the course of that emphasis went awry. Sad to say, the dilution of doctrine and the diminishing of discipline were often undertaken in the name of the Council.

Nothing is more enlightening than to recall the exact words of the Council. These are the words of Pope John XXIII on the opening day, words with which he spelled out the meaning of the Council: "The greatest concern of the Ecumenical Council is this, that the sacred deposit of Christian doctrine should be more effectively guarded and taught." The Pope used these words to set the tone of the Council, the orientation of this great event in the modern history of the Church. His was a great vision, and it forms the only valid way and sound basis for an Ecumenical Council which is aimed at pastoral renewal. It is the only foundation for the care of souls—they must know the truth of Christ.

Pope John Paul II restates the purpose: "This then is my own deepest hope for the pastors of the Church in America, as well as for all the pastors of the Universal Church: that the sacred deposit of Christian doctrine should be more effectively guarded and taught." Perhaps those words should be engraved over the entrance of all of our churches. This sacred deposit is the joy and the strength of our people's lives. It is the only solution that the pastors of souls can bring to the problems that beset our people. The greatest service we can render the people is to present this sacred deposit of Christian doctrine in all its integrity and purity. They are disserved by half truths, if I may be so bold.

The second hope for our day is to maintain intact the discipline of the Church in our own lives as priests and in the lives of our people. The history of the Church has experienced the fruits of this discipline throughout the centuries. The examples of holiness bear sufficient witness as does the service to the poor.

It is no wonder that the Pope places his hopes for the life of the Church in purity of doctrine and sound discipline. He has to depend on this generation to transmit it to the young—the Church's commitment to the Gospel, especially the doctrine of the cross as explained by Luke in his ninth chapter (Lk. 9:23-26).

I hope for a new emphasis on the importance of doctrine and discipline as a post-conciliar contribution to our seminaries. We have a sacred responsibility to lead the People of God "in right paths for his name's sake" (Ps. 23:3).

I remember years ago attending the first Mass of a priest when I was not yet twenty years of age. The preacher was noted for his eloquence, and he ended with the beautiful words from John 17:12: "As long as I was with them, I guarded them with your name which you gave me. I kept careful watch, and not one of them was lost." I remembered those words, and I see now "the careful watch" exemplified in the Pope in 2D.

The fundamental quality of Pope John Paul II is the depth of his faith, which is a reasoned faith.... The new Pope not only believes but he can explain his belief. Pope John Paul II has an overwhelming love for man, for every man, not excluding sinners and the errant. And he's had to deal with them in Poland, even communists. He has never looked at them in any other way except as the image and likeness of God. While, as of this moment, they are in error, he never lets this color his obligation to teach them the truth. Even though they are card-carrying communists, he regards them as ours, as his children.

John Cardinal Krol
Archbishop of Philadelphia

SECTION FIVE

The Journey of the Pope

19 Go Simply to the People

One of the things that has always confused our people is the position of the Church in politics, the "Render to Caesar" quotation. How far and when should we intervene before things get too bad or out of hand completely?

Once again, Pope John Paul II, during the Latin American pilgrimage, came to our assistance in as clear a way as we have heard. Admittedly, the position of the Church in Latin America has claimed the attention of many Popes. The Latin Americans are vastly different from us North Americans in economics and in culture. Since this was the Pope's first major visit outside the Vatican, he must have considered it to be an important question. On the initial day of that trip, Pope John Paul II told a reporter, "The Church and politics is a big question. I think it is necessary to go simply to the people as they are. It is always man who is most important." Of course, this is the Pope's basic thesis—man; this is his great concern over the years. This is the solution of a Pope who comes from a Communist country and has witnessed the suppression of the rights of man first hand.

The Pope said fundamentally that political liberation comes from liberation from sin. We should not be as much concerned about political ideologies, but more about Christ's love for all men.

It is good to be reminded that Jesus was not a political figure, not a revolutionary as some have taught, not a subversive person, not one involved in the class struggle.

"So the distinctive vocation and deepest identity of the Church is the mission to evangelize." The Church is the Church of the people. It is not to be considered first as an institution, "the official Church." Many people in recent years have turned their backs on the official Church as though it were against the needs of people. The Pope said that the "first and foremost concern of the Church is truth about man."

What the Pope was doing among the Latin Americans was what has to be done throughout the world—perhaps warn our bishops, priests, and religious to stay out of partisan politics and concern themselves

primarily with their priesthood and religious life. However, it is our role as priests
to encourage the people, to be "spiritual
guides who must endeavor to orient and
better the hearts of the faithful so that con-
verted, they live the love of God and neigh-
bor and commit themselves to the welfare
and dignity of men."

Our role as priests is to form a social
conscience at all levels. Let the people themselves implement the Church's social teachings. Rather than involve themselves in
politics, the priest must see that the people
are informed. In other words "catechesis"
is still the great work of the ecclesial family.

We are in debt to Pope John Paul II for a
concrete direction for our parish commu-
nities—clearly stated.

It is a question of the highest importance
that in internal social life as well as in international life, all human beings in every nation
and country should be able to enjoy effectively
their full rights under any political regime or
system. Only the safeguarding of this real com-
pleteness of rights for every human being, without discrimination, can insure peace at its very
roots.

Pope John Paul II
At the United Nations

20 Sto Lat

Certainly the Pope wanted to return home to assure his countrymen that God has called them as well as him to a special mission.

He had his ticket to return home right after the conclave, but his election changed his plans. He laid his homeland on the altar of sacrifice for all. Yet, he did want the Polish people to see the first Polish Pope— they deserved that honor, especially those who would never find it possible to come to Rome. There is something warm and compassionate about this special homecoming.

The Pope's original plan was to return to Poland in May for the feast of St. Stanislaus who is buried under the cathedral in Krakow, the Pope's former church. The government feared the overtones of the Pope's taking on somewhat of the role of the saint who had opposed the ruling authorities. So they asked him to postpone his return until June which he did. Whereupon, rather cleverly, the Pope, by a special papal decree, extended the solemn observance of the feast until June.

The homecoming was tumultuous. The Polish people could not have done more to show their joy, their pride, and their gratitude to God for their native son.

John Paul II was never more eloquent. On several occasions, his voice reached very high points of fervor and then fell off into a whisper. He was frequently overcome by emotion as when turning to address his brother bishops on one occasion, he was unable to return to the microphone for several minutes. Of course, this showed to the world the very human Polish Pope.

The main theme of the visit was the role of the East and the West in Christ's economy. He wanted to emphasize that the East must make its contribution known now that we have a Slavic Pope, and that the Polish people have received a special mission from Christ as has their native son.

You cannot help but feel close to a Pope who simply wants his compatriots to be proud that God has so loved their country. You cannot help but love a Pope who simply wants to be among his compatriots and to pray with them and at their familiar shrines. You cannot help but love a people who sing, cheer, wave papal flags, line the highway for hours, strew flowers along the white lines in the middle of the road, walk hours long to see their Pope. And, of course, you must weep with them as they burst in-to Sto-Lat, "may he live a hundred years," and they mean it!

"This Slav Pope"

Nothing in Pope John Paul II's dramatically successful homecoming to Poland sent shock waves rippling across the Soviet empire more surely than his constant reference to himself as "this Slav Pope."

It was a supremely calculated, disarmingly simple statement that reached deep into the psyche of Eastern Europe's hostage populations. It touched a nerve that is peculiarly Slavic, an intangible expression of brotherhood and fierce loyalties that Westerners have been able to glimpse only through the writings of such men as Dostoevski, Tolstoy, Chekhov and, more recently, Solzhenitsyn.

Indeed, one of the recurring topics in Solzhenitsyn's writings is that a Christian missionary would one day emerge from behind the Iron Curtain to set his own people free and breathe new life into Christianity throughout the world. That John Paul is that missionary in the hearts and minds of millions of Slavs, there is little doubt.

Words hardly do justice to the enthusiastic outpouring that greeted the Holy Father every step of the way during his nine-day pilgrimage in Poland. Seasoned foreign correspondents from the West were seen to weep at the powerful emotions John Paul unleashed among the millions of Poles who thronged to see him.

Beyond the borders of Poland, the impact of the papal visit was equally electric, even though there was an almost total blackout of news in the state-controlled media. Public demonstrations of faith, spontaneous examples of—

EUROCATHOLICISM

—blossomed like summer flowers throughout the Soviet orbit in places like Lithuania, the Ukraine, Hungary, Czechoslovakia and Romania despite the not-so-subtle efforts of government officials to discourage them.

It is obvious that the Catholic faith is alive and vigorously healthy behind the Iron Curtain, 35 years of suppression and indoctrination notwithstanding. But there is something more.

John Paul's triumphant return to Poland went considerably beyond the adulation of a Catholic people for the first Polish Pope. The exuberant expression of faith in their Church is the Polish people's way of affirming that their first loyalties belong to something infinitely higher than the state.

Poland, like her Slav sisters, remains a daughter of the Church. And that is something before which tanks and Marxist-Leninist propaganda are powerless.

The Daily News
June 7, 1979

21

A Time of Sadness

The details of the Pope's beautiful visit to Ireland, the first Pope ever to visit that country, are chronicled. What underlies these details is the Pope's sadness at something that has been part of the climate of the Church for this last decade.

It occurred on his last day in the Emerald Isle, October 1, 1979. It took place at the revered Irish seminary of world renown, Maynooth. He first pleaded with the priests and religious to be "signs of God" and to be faithful to their religious commitments.

"Do not hesitate to be recognizable, identifiable, in the streets as men and women who have consecrated their lives to God."

It was certain that the Pope felt a sorrow because some have abandoned their religious habits for various reasons. He feels that the witness value has been lost, and the hesitation to be recognizable and identifiable has hurt the people more than it has helped them.

He also knows the confusion of the laity and their disappointments with the clerical state. "If you keep striving to be the kind of priests your people expect and wish you to be, then you will be holy priests." He does want priests to meet the expectations of the devout laity—he knows that we seldom rise above their ideal but it must remain an ideal. Their great expectations can bring us to great holiness, and we are caught in the grasp of their love for the priesthood.

The Pope then draws the sad conclusion: "This is what causes such sadness to the Church, such great but often silent anguish among the People of God, when priests fail in their fidelity to their priestly commitment."

The Pope has heard the silent anguish of the People of God when their priests abandon their commitment. He has felt the sorrows of the down decade of the 70's when the number of departures was amazingly 2,000 a year. God needs men and He chooses them. We are free and we consent. The People of God rejoice in the call, and they cannot take easily the failure to make the consent a permanent one.

The Pope knows more than he has said, but he has said a great deal in a few words about a time of sadness that has confused and disheartened our people. Much of the turmoil is traceable to the diminution of these values, these witness values.

Lord,
source of eternal life and truth,
give to your shepherd John Paul
a spirit of courage and right judgment,
a spirit of knowledge and love.
By governing with fidelity those entrusted to his
    care
may he, as Successor to the apostle Peter and
    Vicar of Christ,
build your Church into a sacrament of unity,
    love, and peace for all the world.
We ask this through our Lord Jesus Christ,
    your son,
who lives and reigns with you and the Holy
    Spirit,
one God, for ever and ever. Amen.

22 Look to Christ

Any words that I may write could in no way bespeak the love of the Holy Father for youth as perfectly as what follows. This is a classic in every respect. It was spoken to high school students, October 3, 1979, in Madison Square Garden, New York.

Dear young people,

I am happy to be with you in Madison Square Garden. Today this is a garden of life, where young people are alive: alive with hope and love, alive with the life of Christ. And it is in the name of Christ that I greet each one of you today.

I have been told that most of you come from Catholic high schools. For this reason I would like to say something about Catholic education, to tell you why the Church considers it so important and expends so much energy in order to provide you and millions of other young people with a Catholic education. The answer can be summarized in one word, in one Person, Jesus Christ. The Church wants to communicate Christ to you.

This is what education is all about, this is the meaning of life: to know Christ. To know Christ as a friend, as someone who cares about you and the person next to you, and all the people here and everywhere—no matter what language they speak, or what clothes they wear, or what color their skin is.

And so the purpose of Catholic education is to communicate Christ to you, so that your attitude toward others will be that of Christ. You are approaching that stage in your life when you must take personal responsibility for your own destiny. Soon you will be making major decisions which will affect the whole course of your life. If these decisions reflect Christ's attitude, your education will be a success.

We have to learn to meet challenges and even crises in the light of Christ's cross and resurrection. Part of our Catholic education is to learn to see the needs of others, to have the courage to practice what we believe in. With the support of a Catholic education we try to meet every circumstance of life with the attitude of

Christ. Yes, the Church wants to communicate Christ to you so that you will come to full maturity in Him who is the perfect human being, and at the same time the Son of God.

Dear young people, you and I and all of us together make up the Church, and we are convinced that only in Christ do we find real love, and the fullness of life.

And so I invite you today to look to Christ.

When you wonder about the mystery of yourself, look to Christ who gives you the meaning of life.

When you wonder what it means to be a mature person, look to Christ who is the fullness of humanity.

And when you wonder about your role in the future of the world and of the United States, look to Christ. Only in Christ will you fulfill your potential as an American citizen and as a citizen of the world community.

With the aid of your Catholic education, you have received the greatest of gifts: "I believe nothing can happen that will outweigh the supreme advantage of knowing Christ Jesus my Lord. For him I have accepted the loss of everything and I look on everything as so much rubbish if only I can have Christ and be given a place in him" (Phil. 3:8-9).

Be always grateful to God for this gift of knowing Christ. Be grateful also to your parents and to the community of the Church for making possible, through many sacrifices, your Catholic education. People have placed a lot of hope in you and they now look forward to your collaboration in giving witness to Christ, and in transmitting the Gospel to others. The Church needs you. The world needs you, because it needs Christ, and you belong to Christ. And so I ask you to accept your responsibility in the Church, the responsibility of your Catholic education: to help—by your words, and, above all, by the example of your lives—to spread the Gospel. You do this by praying, and by being just and truthful and pure.

Dear young people: by a real Christian life, by the practice of your religion you are called to give witness to your Faith. And because actions speak louder than words, you are called to proclaim by the conduct of your daily lives that you really do believe that Jesus Christ is Lord!

Keep Jesus Christ in your hearts, and you
will recognize His face in every human being.
You will want to help Him out in all His needs:
the needs of your brothers and sisters.

Pope John Paul II
Shea Stadium

23 God Bless America

Boston, New York, United Nations, Philadelphia, Des Moines, Chicago, Washington, all resounded "John Paul II—we love you." To which the Pope replied "John Paul II—he loves you!"

The events of the pilgrimage of faith to America will never be forgotten by the millions who witnessed them in person or, thanks be to God, via television. The Church needed a boost in America and this was it. Our faith was renovated.

The Pope stopped time. Millions followed him. Everyone else was glued to television for the seven days so as not to miss a thing. He enthralled children and transfixed a nation. His personal love touched the hearts of all, the reaction being greater than he imagined. Both were amazed at how this non-Catholic country responded. Karol Wojtyla had been here before in 1969 and 1976 for extended weeks, but never as Pope. The people now took him to their hearts as the Vicar of Christ. As he crossed the Atlantic Ocean on his way here from Ireland, he must have been praying for this. His prayers were heard.

Will his message be remembered? Will his words be taken to heart? Will people differentiate between his person and his message! I hope not, because they are intertwined. His own faith and love told us to love our faith, to love our Church. His own love of America, whose ground he kissed as he came down from the airplane, told us to love America the beautiful, to which he so often referred. ("Beautiful—even when it rains"—as it so often did during the visit.)

His own fierce devotion to truth told us to seek the truth and to guard it with sacred force. His own clinging to the permanent things told us that there are certain fundamental laws which preserve the dignity of man as God's chief work. His own serene courage in the face of the turmoil of the last ten years gives us courage to confront the sign of contradiction between the laws of God and the liberal demands of a decaying morality. His offering of Mass in each of his places of pastoral visitation was exquisitely beautiful, bringing strength and solace to those who lament the loss of the sacred.

We priests have often felt we are fighting a losing battle; we were afraid. Now, the Pope reaffirmed our priestly dedication to Christ and encouraged our faith beyond anything we had hoped for. We are not afraid. We appreciate him as a gift from God.

The young people responded to him unbelievably, and they saw a man of faith and love and hope. He made the Pope someone real. They previously thought they might neither understand him nor his pronunciation—he made sure they did. Some of the children, when they grow up, will be told that the Pope kissed them and held them—a blessing beyond description.

So a large part of his message is part of the Holy Father himself. The Pope called us "his very dear children," when he returned to Rome. He is our very dear Father.

He gave more than fifty talks, some of them an hour in length, yet nobody seemed to mind. We hung on every word—amazed that he could master our language and read our hearts; a miracle in itself! He was strong in teaching the Word of God with no equivocation or compromise: "I propose to you the option of love which is the opposite of escape.... Do not be afraid of honest effort and honest work; do not be afraid of the truth."

"It behooves the theologian to be free but with the freedom that is openness to the truth and the light that comes from faith and from fidelity to the Church." That last is a key phrase—"fidelity to the Church," the voice of Christ among us.

The moral issues were restated traditionally based on the standards of moral conduct that should be accepted by all. New York City, now known as the Big Apple, had souvenir sticker big apples in red with "Welcome, Pope John Paul II" printed on them. Someone brought me two of them which I pasted on two lamp shades in our home.

There were many other souvenirs far more costly. Yet these two simple New York stickers say it all. You are forever welcome, Pope John Paul II! We need you! We'll leave the stickers on the lampshades as they are. That is our way of saying that you will linger forever in our hearts and in our homes.

America has opened her heart to me. And now I must leave the United States and return to Rome. But all of you will constantly be remembered in my prayers, which I look upon as the best expression of my loyalty and friendship.

Today, therefore, my final prayer is this: That God will bless America, so that she may increasingly become and truly be and long remain, "one nation, under God, indivisible, with liberty and justice for all."

God bless America!
God bless America!

Pope John Paul II

Epilogue

Much will be written about the future of the Church. The pastoral ministry of John Paul II will be discussed by experts. Many of us do not understand the deep complexities that will confront the Pope. Many of us do understand the Pope. We know that he believes he has a God-given mission to lead the Church through its troubles and to reconcile the divisions. We firmly believe that is why Christ called this surprisingly extraordinary Pope. The Pope has the assurance of that same call. Prayerfully he will bring the Church to the third millennium and perhaps beyond.

All over the world, people are thanking God and Mary, the Mother of the Church, for the Pope. This priest now thanks God for the gift of Pope John Paul II and thanks Pope John Paul II for reminding him of the gifts of God.

Reverend Monsignor John F. Davis

1920	Born February 3, 1920, Jersey City, N.J.
1925-1935	Attended Public Schools, Jersey City, N.J.
1935	Graduated Seton Hall Preparatory School, S. Orange, N.J.
1939	Awarded A.B., Seton Hall College, S. Orange, N.J.
1943	Awarded Licentiate in Sacred Theology (S.T.L.) Catholic University, Washington, D.C.
1943	Ordained Priest for Archdiocese of Newark, N.J.
1943-1947	Associate Pastor and Instuctor of English, Holy Trinity Church, Westfield, N.J.
1947-1963	Vice President in charge of Business Affairs and Instructor of Economics and Theology, Seton Hall University
1950	Awarded M.B.A., New York University, Graduate School of Business Administration Thesis—The Alberta Experiment in Social Credit

1955	Author *Catholic Transcription Studies* (Textbook)
1962	Named Papal Chamberlain by Pope John XXIII
1962-1969	Director, Society for the Propagation of the Faith, Archdiocese of Newark
	Weekly Columnist "The Advocate," Archdiocesan Newspaper
1969-	Pastor, St. Michael's Church, Cranford, N.J.

Also available:

U.S.A.—THE MESSAGE OF JUSTICE, PEACE AND LOVE

Complete collection of the talks given by His Holiness, Pope John Paul II, during his historic visit to America, October 1-7, 1979: Boston, New York, Philadelphia, Des Moines, Chicago, Washington. What did the Vicar of Christ tell America wherever he went? A book to treasure, to meditate, to live by. 320 pages; cloth $5.95; paper $4.95 — EP1095

POPE JOHN PAUL II— HE CAME TO US AS A FATHER

A **pictorial volume** in full color. Covers the entire visit of the Holy Father to the United States, from arrival through tour, to departure. A unique book on a unique historical event. A book of memories which, while recalling happy events, fosters spiritual renewal. 256 pages, over 300 full-color photographs, 100 black and white; gift edition $14.95 — EP0957

PUEBLA—A PILGRIMAGE OF FAITH

The 36 talks of Pope John Paul II given during his Latin American pilgrimage.

11 photographs in black and white — 208 pages; paper $2.00 — EP0976

PILGRIM TO POLAND

A collection of the Holy Father's 41 talks given during his heartwarming visit to his native Poland. 54 photographs in color and black and white — 290 pages; cloth $5.00; paper $3.50 — EP0955

TURKEY—ECUMENICAL PILGRIMAGE

"That they may be one, even as we are one" (Jn. 17:11). The talks of the 2-day visit to Turkey. 14 color photos and 10 black and white. An historic book. 112 pages; cloth $3.50; paper $2.50 — EP1085

AFRICA—APOSTOLIC PILGRIMAGE

Contains all 72 talks of John Paul II during his 10-day visit to the people of Africa.

Thought-provoking for all the people of God. 52 photos in color and black and white; 432 pages; cloth $8.00; paper $7.00 — EP0025

FRANCE—MESSAGE OF PEACE, TRUST, LOVE AND FAITH

The 28 addresses in the Pope's 4-day visit to France, a "country of glorious tradition." 37 photographs; 250 pages; cloth $5.00; paper $3.50 — EP0488

IRELAND—"IN THE FOOTSTEPS OF ST. PATRICK"

Pope John Paul II's historic 3-day visit to Ireland is recaptured in this collection of 22 talks given by His Holiness from September 29 to October 1, 1979.

The Holy Father's message is one of peace and reconciliation, justice and respect among all peoples, and tells of the Pope's great love for "Ireland always faithful." 141 pages; cloth $3.95; paper $2.95 — EP0675

"YOU ARE THE FUTURE YOU ARE MY HOPE"

Talks of John Paul II **to young people** of all ages, from his papal election to the present. Reveals the stirring personal appeal of the Pope to the new generation. Excellent for youth and those involved in guidance. 326 pages, 16 pages of full-color photos; cloth $4.95; paper $3.95 — EP1120

VISIBLE SIGNS OF THE GOSPEL

Messages of John Paul II on consecrated life. Faith, warmth and encouragement read in his every word. 308 pages; cloth $4.00; paper $2.95 — EP1098

APOSTOLIC EXHORTATION ON CATECHESIS IN OUR TIME
(Catechesi Tradendae)

68 pages; 60¢ — EP0185

"YOU ARE MY FAVORITES"
Pope John Paul II to children
Edited by the Daughters of St. Paul

In this colorful book, full of pictures and photographs, the Pope speaks to all the children of the world. He tells them about Jesus, faith, love, truth, school, holidays, sports, the Gospel, and much, much more. 192 pages; cloth $6.95 — EP1125

THE REDEEMER OF MAN

Encyclical Letter. **Redemptor Hominis,** March 4, 1978, the first of His Holiness' pontificate. 64 pages; 50¢ — EP0978Z

BRAZIL—JOURNEY IN THE LIGHT OF THE EUCHARIST

Pope John Paul II made a 12-day pilgrimage to the largest Catholic country in the world (June 30—

July 11, 1980). He delivered 54 addresses before departure, during the pilgrimage and upon his return. They are collected in this volume. 37 pictures capture high points in this historic event.

The Pope's message was universal, filled with warmth and understanding, reflecting sensitivity to the needs of all people. cloth $8.00; paper $7.00 — EP0175

Daughters of St. Paul

IN MASSACHUSETTS
    50 St. Paul's Ave. Jamaica Plain, Boston, MA 02130;
        617-522-8911; 617-522-0875;
    172 Tremont Street, Boston, MA 02111; **617-426-5464;**
        617-426-4230
IN NEW YORK
    78 Fort Place, Staten Island, NY 10301; **212-447-5071**
    59 East 43rd Street, New York, NY 10017; **212-986-7580**
    7 State Street, New York, NY 10004; **212-447-5071**
    625 East 187th Street, Bronx, NY 10458; **212-584-0440**
    525 Main Street, Buffalo, NY 14203; **716-847-6044**
IN NEW JERSEY
    Hudson Mall — Route 440 and Communipaw Ave.,
        Jersey City, NJ 07304; **201-433-7740**
IN CONNECTICUT
    202 Fairfield Ave., Bridgeport, CT 06604; **203-335-9913**
IN OHIO
    2105 Ontario St. (at Prospect Ave.), Cleveland, OH 44115; **216-621-9427**
    25 E. Eighth Street, Cincinnati, OH 45202; **513-721-4838**
IN PENNSYLVANIA
    1719 Chestnut Street, Philadelphia, PA 19103; **215-568-2638**
IN FLORIDA
    2700 Biscayne Blvd., Miami, FL 33137; **305-573-1618**
IN LOUISIANA
    4403 Veterans Memorial Blvd., Metairie, LA 70002; **504-887-7631;**
        504-887-0113
    1800 South Acadian Thruway, P.O. Box 2028, Baton Rouge, LA 70821
        504-343-4057; 504-343-3814
IN MISSOURI
    1001 Pine Street (at North 10th), St. Louis, MO 63101; **314-621-0346;**
        314-231-1034
IN ILLINOIS
    172 North Michigan Ave., Chicago, IL 60601; **312-346-4228**
IN TEXAS
    114 Main Plaza, San Antonio, TX 78205; **512-224-8101**
IN CALIFORNIA
    1570 Fifth Avenue, San Diego, CA 92101; **714-232-1442**
    46 Geary Street, San Francisco, CA 94108; **415-781-5180**
IN HAWAII
    1143 Bishop Street, Honolulu, HI 96813; **808-521-2731**
IN ALASKA
    750 West 5th Avenue, Anchorage AK 99501; **907-272-8183**
IN CANADA
    3022 Dufferin Street, Toronto 395, Ontario, Canada
IN ENGLAND
    128, Notting Hill Gate, London W11 3QG, England
    133 Corporation Street, Birmingham B4 6PH, England
    5A-7 Royal Exchange Square, Glasgow G1 3AH, England
    82 Bold Street, Liverpool L1 4HR, England
IN AUSTRALIA
    58 Abbotsford Rd., Homebush, N.S.W., Sydney 2140, Australia